# Vishal Sharma
# William Jaworski

ALTAMIRA STUDIO
2024

ASK ARISTOTLE. Copyright © 2024 by Vishal Sharma and William Jaworski.

All rights reserved.

First published 2024 by Altamira Studio.

No part of this publication may be reproduced, stored in a retrieval system, or transmitted, in any form or by any means, without the prior written permission of the authors, or as expressly permitted by law. Enquiries concerning reproduction outside the scope of the above should be sent to the authors.

You must not circulate this book in any other binding or over and you must impose the same condition on any acquirer.

Translations from Greek and Latin are William Jaworski's own.

Paperback ISBN: 979-8-9901472-0-1
eBook ISBN: 979-8-9901472-1-8

*To our children*

# Preface

An unexpected trip got us talking about Aristotle—and death, money, wisdom, and the struggle to be fulfilled in life. We thought it would be fun to write the story of that trip from Vishal's point of view.

We're grateful to Michelle Madrid, Susanna Cates, Francisco Rodriguez Solana, Quay Bangs, Phuong Le, Paul Coleman, and Sean Green for their support and encouragement.

# 1

We ate the mushrooms. Thirty minutes later we were under the covers, laughing at our silly banter, the bed sheet making a translucent roof over our heads. "I'll be right back," she said and slipped out.

I was alone. Little by little, I felt like something was pressing in on me from all sides. "*I'm going to die*," I thought, "*Here. By myself. In the bed.*" I called out from under the sheet, "Michelle, are you there?"

"I'm just using the bathroom," her voice came from the next room.

"Can you come back? You've been gone a long time."

"I'm right here," she said, crawling back under the covers.

"I think I'm going to die."

She was calm: "Remember what Henry said." Henry was a friend who'd worked as a facilitator for psychedelic experiences. I'd told him my wife and I were planning a weekend getaway to Joshua Tree and might try some psychedelics. I asked his advice. 'If you start freaking out,' he said, 'go into nature, touch the ground, and take some deep breaths.' "Let's go outside," Michelle said, "you'll feel better."

We threw off the covers and stepped outside. The desert surrounded us. The air was a crisp forty degrees. "Maybe a bath?" she said. Our room had an outdoor tub. I turned on the tap. I was in a cold sweat. The landscape looked like an image from another planet—an unforgiving world with toxic air. I watched the water level rise in the tub. "*One of us could drown!*" I thought. I cut the water.

I glimpsed my reflection in the glass of a window. It was eerie and spectral. "*Am I already dead?*" The kids were safe at home with my mother. What would she tell them? I started feeling afraid—not of death, but of embarrassment. I curled up on the bed in a fetal position. Would we be one of those couples you hear about who try a drug and accidentally kill themselves? I had an image of my friend Ben talking to his wife in their refurbished kitchen, his eyes wide with shock, peering over the top of his phone: 'Vishal and Michelle took some psychedelics. They died!'

"Call Henry!" I said.

"I already did," Michelle said, "It's going straight to voicemail."

I needed someone to help me work through this. Who else could guide me? "Call Bill!" Bill was a professional philosopher.

Michelle dialed. I heard snippets of conversation: "…mushrooms… freaking out a bit… no, nothing like that… maybe just talk to him…" She handed me the phone, "It's Bill."

I heard Bill's voice: "Hey, Vishal. What's up?"

"I can't stop thinking about death."

"What are you thinking about it?"

"I don't want to die."

"Okay. Let's start with that. Why don't you want to die?"

What a bizarre question! It took me a minute to answer. "I want to raise my kids," I said. "They're the most important thing to me. I want to be there for them. I want… I want… to teach them."

"Okay. What do you want to teach them?" Bill said.

What was it that I wanted to teach them? I wasn't sure. I tried thinking about it, but nothing came into my head. Instead an answer seemed to well up out of my chest: "I want to teach them how to live!" I paused. Now that I'd said it out loud, I realized I had no idea how to teach someone to live. What exactly were you supposed to say or do? Did Bill know? I'd worked with him on things like logic, critical thinking, and cognitive biases. But we'd never talked about philosophy. "Bill, do you know how to live?" I asked.

"I'm figuring it out like everyone else," he said.

"But you have a PhD."

He gave a short laugh. "All that means is that I have a lot of stamina for a certain kind of mental work. But okay, sure: I've been studying the matter a long time."

"I haven't been studying it a long time," I said. "But I've been wondering about it a long time."

"Tell me about that," he said. "Do you remember when you first started wondering?"

Memories began racing through my mind, one after another. It felt like I was being transported into a scene from my past, just a few years ago. I was in bed, my body shaking with sobs. The red digits of the bedside clock looked blurry through my tears: 3:23 a.m. Michelle stirred in the bed beside me, 'Vishal, my love, what's the matter?'

The scene from my memory seemed more real to me than my actual surroundings. I heard Bill's voice, as if he were standing next to me, the two of us watching my past self in the bed, "Tell me where we are, Vishal." I explained the background to him. My father had died a few months earlier. I used to take him to his dialysis sessions. I'd rub his feet to ease his muscle cramps, and we'd talk. I'd often ask him for advice, and on one occasion, I asked him about death.

"What did he say?" Bill said.

"He said, 'Always go to funerals, and always visit people in the hospital. The hard times: that's when real friends show up.'"

"Sounds right."

"Yeah, but that's not what I'm getting at," I said. "The thing is, he never told me how to handle losing someone you love. He once talked about his own father's death. My grandfather died when my father was just seventeen. My father had to take over the family business and care for his mother and siblings. 'One day you'll know what it feels like to lose your father,' he said. That was it. That was the closest he got to talking about losing someone you love."

"What's the connection between those conversations with your father and this scene with you waking up in the middle of the night?" Bill said.

"I suppose my dad gave me the impression that when you lose someone, you just put grief to one side and move on. I'd been reading a lot of Stoic philosophers at the time. They gave me the same impression: don't be troubled by things that aren't in your control—like death. People die. You can't control that. I knew my father was dying. And after he died, I knew I couldn't bring him back. These were things I couldn't control. So I never wept—not when he was on life support, not in his final moments, not at his funeral. I kept thinking, 'I have to control the controllable.' I thought I had it managed. But now, months later, you see me here in this scene, weeping in the middle of the night."

The scene shifted again. I was transported into a different memory from around the same time in my past. I was walking into my house, a smile on my face. My mother was there cooking. Bill and I watched the scene unfold. The smile on my face faded. I left the kitchen and sat alone.

"What's happening here?" Bill said.

"I'd had a good day. I walked into the house. It smelled amazing! I could tell what my mother was cooking. It was my father's favorite dish. It got me thinking about him. I started to feel… just… empty."

The scene shifted again. I was at work reading an email. Bill and I watched as my past self started to smile and laugh. "It's good news," I explained. We watched as my past self reached for the phone, then stopped, with a look on his face as if he might be sick. "My father and I were both businessmen," I said. "It was one of the interests we shared. When something good happened at work, he was often the first person I'd call. I was just about to call him. Then I remembered he was dead."

The scene shifted yet again. Michelle and my past self were in the middle of an argument. "This was so stupid," I said with embarrassment, "I don't even remember what it was about. I just… it happened a lot around this time."

"What happened a lot?" Bill said.

"I had a short fuse. The littlest things would set me off. I felt so frustrated! I was trying so hard to be stoic." Bill was silent. I started feeling foolish. "Do you have any idea what I'm talking about?" I said.

"Maybe," said Bill. "Can I share an observation that might help explain these episodes?"

"Tell me."

"Stoic philosophy misunderstands human emotions. It tries eliminating them. The Stoic philosopher Seneca put it this way:

> It is often asked whether it is better to have moderate emotions or none. Our people expel the emotions; the Peripatetics moderate them.[1]

"The Peripatetics were followers of Aristotle. Aristotle knew that eliminating emotions is impossible for biological beings like us. His philosophy aims at training or disciplining emotions—channeling their energy, harnessing them so we can live better lives. But Seneca says that's not the aim of Stoicism. Stoicism doesn't aim at training or disciplining emotions but expelling them. Cicero applies this idea to grief—the very emotion you struggled with when your father died. He sees grief as an evil, a weakness—he even calls it a disease.[2] You don't train or moderate diseases, you eliminate them. So Cicero rejects the idea of training or moderating the emotions, just as Seneca does. Grief, he says, is for cowards; it's fundamentally about fearing something evil, like death. To grieve, he

---

[1] Utrum satius sit modicos habere adfectus an nullos saepe quaesitum est. Nostri illos expellunt, Peripatetici temperant (*Ad Lucilium Epistulae Morales*, letter 116).

[2] *Tusculan Disputations*, book 3.

says, is to cower in the face of what's fearful, and cowering in fear is something a wise and virtuous person would never do."

"Do you think he's right about grief?" I asked.

"On the contrary, I think it's clear he's wrong. Grief isn't fundamentally about fearing something evil; it's about losing something good. Grief is painful—that's true. But many good things are: exercising, apologizing, forgiving, loving. What sets apart wise and virtuous people isn't immunity to grief. Loss visits everyone—sages and fools alike. What sets apart wise and virtuous people is that they grieve the loss of things that are genuinely good, and their grief leaves them grateful for that goodness. It isn't courage to avoid grieving the loss of good things. On the contrary, it's courage to embrace the pain of their loss. Courage endures hardship for the sake of something valuable. What's valuable in grief is the opportunity to appreciate and be grateful for the good thing you've lost. To avoid grief is to avoid gratitude. You cherished your father, and you cherished his memory. But you were trying to be stoic, and Stoic practice had you avoiding the experience of grief. But in avoiding grief, you were also avoiding gratitude, and that made things doubly painful: it hurt to lose your father, and it hurt not to allow yourself to feel gratitude for his life."

"But I thought Stoics were all about gratitude."

"They are," Bill continued, "that's one of the ironies of Stoicism—a tension between Stoic theory and Stoic practice. Stoic theory promotes gratitude, but Stoic practice does just the opposite. It aims at disconnecting you from the world emotionally to avoid the pain of loss. The Stoic philosopher Epictetus put it this way:

> With each thing that delights you, or that is useful, or that you love, remember to tell yourself what kind of thing it is, beginning with the smallest things. If, for instance, you love a cup, remember that it is merely a cup you love, for then you won't be troubled if it breaks; if you kiss your child or wife, remember that it is merely something human you kiss, for then you won't be troubled if he or she dies.[3]

"The goal of practicing what Epictetus says is to achieve a state in which you won't be troubled by terrible losses like the death of people you love. But there are at least two problems with the practice.

"First, it's not clear that you can really achieve the emotional numbness it aims at. You can imagine, say, the death of your child as much as you want. But how much will that blunt the edge of real loss if your child dies and

---

3 ἐφ᾽ ἑκάστου τῶν ψυχαγωγούντων ἢ χρείαν παρεχόντων ἢ στεργομένων μέμνησο ἐπιλέγειν, ὁποῖόν ἐστιν, ἀπὸ τῶν σμικροτάτων ἀρξάμενος· ἂν χύτραν στέργῃς, ὅτι 'χύτραν στέργω.' κατεαγείσης γὰρ αὐτῆς οὐ ταραχθήσῃ· ἂν παιδίον σαυτοῦ καταφιλῇς ἢ γυναῖκα, ὅτι ἄνθρωπον καταφιλεῖς· ἀποθανόντος γὰρ οὐ ταραχθήσῃ. (*Enchiridion*, chapter 3).

you can't retreat from your dark imaginings to the world in which your child still lives? Just ask yourself: how much did Stoic practice blunt the edge of losing your father?

"Second, the practice encourages a kind of delusion. It has you pretending you aren't surrounded by good things you should be grateful for—ignoring the real world with good things in favor of an imagined world without them. Practicing ingratitude and delusion is neither courageous nor wise. Courage doesn't run from the pain of loss, and wisdom doesn't blind itself to real things that warrant our gratitude."

"So wait," I said, "you're saying—when you talk about the irony of Stoicism—what you mean is, Stoicism says one thing but does another? Like it says, 'be courageous, and wise, and grateful,' but then it has you doing things that make you the opposite?"

"That's right," Bill said. "Don't get me wrong: sometimes imagining something's loss can help you see a good thing you've been taking for granted. But ruminating on possible loss at length can go awry if it doesn't aim at gratitude, and the practice that Stoics like Epictetus promote doesn't aim at gratitude. It aims instead at emotional numbness—at expelling emotions, as Seneca says. If Stoics were right—if grief and other emotions really were diseases—then they'd be right about expelling them. But they're wrong.

"It's true that some things aren't worth grieving. If you falsely believe you're more knowledgeable or competent than you really are, and something shatters that illusion (like underperforming on a task, or encountering someone who knows more), you feel the pain of humiliation—the pain of losing that false image of yourself. The loss of that image isn't worth grieving because that image wasn't really good for you. It actually stood in the way of making better decisions and living a better life. If all we were talking about were cases of losing things that weren't genuinely good, then the Stoics would be right: wise and virtuous people wouldn't grieve their loss any more than they'd grieve losing an addiction or disease. But not everything we lose is bad. Sometimes we lose things that are genuinely good—like your father, someone you loved. We're right to grieve their loss.

"Grieving the loss of good things isn't pathological. It's human—something that happens to social animals with a deep natural desire to love and be loved. If anything is pathological, it's pretending we're not animals of this sort—that we're somehow better off not loving than loving and losing the good things we love. Stoic practice encourages this kind of pretending. It cultivates an attitude that disdains the things we love to avoid the pain of losing them. It tries running from the possibility of emotional injury. It's cowardly in that sense."

"Bill, that's… a lot to think about," I said. "I'm going to need time to process it. Have you written any of this down?"

"Nah."

"Why do you say it like that?"

"Like what?"

"Like you think it's a stupid idea."

"Sorry, I didn't mean to sound that way. It's just nothing I'm saying is new. Objections to Stoicism have been around for two thousand years—including the objections I just rehearsed for you. It's never occurred to me they'd be worth writing down—a bit like reinventing the wheel."

"You know that Stoicism is huge right now?" I said.

"So I've heard," Bill said. "From a philosophical perspective that seems really… weird."

"How so?"

"Well, if you know the history of philosophy, Stoicism just seems like a non-starter. To see someone endorsing it today… it's like seeing someone using an old technology that was abandoned years ago. Like imagine there was some household gadget that people were using in the 1950s, but they discovered it caused cancer, so people stopped using it. Then one day you're cleaning out your attic and find one of those gadgets and decide to use it like people did in the 50s. Anyone familiar with those gadgets would look at you like, 'The fuck you doin'?!' The revival of Stoicism looks like that."

"Do you think maybe it's just that people don't read much philosophy?" I said.

"Maybe," Bill said. "Or maybe they read it but don't understand it. It's hard to understand a philosophical view unless you also understand something about its competitors."

"What do you mean by competitors?"

"I mean other views that try to solve the same problems or answer the same questions but in a different way. Take your question: How should I live? There are different ways of answering that question, and some answers are incompatible with others. For example, Stoicism says that part of the answer is to eliminate emotions. A competing view would say that eliminating emotions isn't part of the answer—that it's instead about training emotions, or giving emotions free rein, or something other than eliminating them. It's harder to evaluate a view if you don't know anything about competing views, just like it's harder to make an informed choice about buying a product if you don't know about the range of competing products that do the same thing."

"So even if people read Seneca or whatever," I said, "they might not understand what they're reading because they don't know about the alternatives to Stoicism?"

"Right," said Bill. "In fairness, they might also be victims of misrepresentation. I've seen people misrepresenting what Stoicism says—trying to revise or sanitize its message. They're analogous to people saying, 'That gadget doesn't cause cancer. It's good for you.'"

"Can you give me an example?"

"Sure. What comes to mind is a quote from Nassim Taleb: 'Stoicism is about the domestication, not necessarily the elimination, of emotions.'[4] Real Stoics like Seneca and Cicero say otherwise. They'll tell you straight up that Stoicism is about eliminating emotions. Domesticating emotions—training or disciplining them—that isn't Stoicism. That's Aristotle."

"Aristotle?"

"Yes," Bill said, "Aristotle. Look, Stoicism doesn't get everything wrong. Not even Aristotle would say that. One of his own principles is that no one is so stupid that they get everything wrong. There's a kernel of truth in what they say. They just surround that kernel with a lot of falsehood. When you evaluate a philosophical theory, part of your job is identifying the kernel of truth it's trying to express, and then extracting that truth from the surrounding falsehoods. So Aristotle says that an accurate account of something can explain what competing views get right in addition to what they get wrong."

"So what does Stoicism get right?"

"The point I mentioned earlier: imagining loss can help you appreciate the good things you have. It's easy to take

---

[4] *Antifragile* (New York: Random House), p. 156.

those things for granted. That's why people say, 'You don't know what you've got till it's gone.' Sometimes just imagining that something is gone can help you understand its value. Some balk at this suggestion. They shudder at the thought of losing good things. They try not to think of loss, and they feel really disturbed when they encounter people who've experienced loss. They prefer the comfort of feeling as if the good things they have can never be lost and hate reminders that those things are fragile. That represents a kind of delusion—one that favors a comfortable falsehood to an uncomfortable truth.

"The practice of imagining loss can help correct that delusion. But you can dwell on potential loss in a way that yields resignation or despair. That's where Stoics like Epictetus go wrong. They imagine loss in an effort to become immune to the pain of it. Their practice encourages a different kind of delusion—not the delusion that things aren't fragile, but the delusion that you aren't surrounded by good things however fragile they are. Gratitude helps avoid that mistake. Think of the beauty of a sunrise, or the birth of your child, or moments in your life when many things came together to yield a precious accomplishment—these things and so many others are fragile and fleeting. But that makes them no less beautiful, no less precious. Their fragility doesn't diminish their value. The practice of gratitude aims at celebrating that value—cherishing good things despite their fragility, being thankful for their presence even if that presence is fleeting."

"So it's like Stoicism starts with the right idea," I said, "but takes it in the wrong direction?"

"You can put it like that. And look: if your only interest in Stoicism is having talking points to share with your friends, then you might not notice its shortcomings. But when you try using it to live life, that's when you'll start noticing its limitations. That's what happened to you. At that point, you might start looking for something better."

"And that better thing is Aristotle?" I said.

"It's one of them," Bill said. "Aristotle definitely has a superior philosophical system."

"What makes it superior?"

"Lots of things. We could talk about them all day. For one thing, it doesn't misunderstand human emotion the way Stoicism does. Even the people who promote Stoicism know there's something wrongheaded about trying to eliminate emotions. That's why they try sanitizing the Stoic message: they make it out that Stoicism is about training emotions instead of eliminating them. But if you read real Stoics like Seneca and Cicero, they say exactly the opposite: they emphasize the goal of eliminating emotions. That's in fact how they distinguish their view from Aristotle's, which aims at training emotions. What I don't understand…" Bill paused. "What really puzzles me, actually… is why today's promoters of Stoicism don't just come clean. They want to reject the real Stoic view, but they don't want to reject the Stoic label. Why not? What's so special about the label? I don't get it."

"I think I might know the answer," I said.

"Really?" Bill sounded skeptical.

"I think," I said, "that Stoicism has become a brand. People have been making money promoting it, so there's now a market for the Stoic product. The people who sell that product can't lose the label without losing the advantage of brand recognition."

Bill was silent.

"Hello? Bill?"

"I'm here, Vishal, sorry. I'm just thinking through the implications of what you've said. So just to be clear… you're saying that people have been using the label 'Stoicism' to sell a product? And in that case, if there's something wrong with the product they've been selling—if, say, it's committed to a wrongheaded view of human emotion—they might change the product formula—for example, they might say it's about training emotions instead of eliminating them—but they won't change the label? They'll continue calling it 'Stoicism' even if it's no longer the same view because they don't want to lose their market share? By analogy, maybe Coca-Cola changed its formula over the years, but no matter what the formula, they still call their product 'Coca-Cola' because if they didn't, they couldn't rely on their established customer base to continue buying their product?"

"Exactly!"

"So if you're right… I've been puzzled by Stoicism's revival because I've been trying to understand it in terms of Stoicism's philosophical merits and demerits. From that perspective, it's not clear why anybody would be attracted to Stoicism because people have known for centuries that it says a bunch of things that are false. But what you're saying is that recent interest in Stoicism has less to do with Stoicism's philosophical merits and more to do with Stoicism's status as a brand—that its revival is a commercial phenomenon not a philosophical one?"

"Yes, that's what I'm saying."

"And something can be a commercial success even if it doesn't work. People buy things that don't work all the time—like weight-loss products. And something similar has happened with Stoicism—or with the product that's been labeled 'Stoicism.' Is that right?"

"Yes."

"Wow! That's a really helpful perspective, Vishal. If you're right, my puzzle is solved. I'm going to have to think more about that. Thank you!" Bill paused for a moment. "But listen," he said, "I want to go back to the question I asked before: the episode when you woke up in the middle of the night, is that the first time you started wondering about how to live?"

"No," I said. "It's just the first thing that came to mind. I'd been wondering about how to live for a long time before that—ever since I was a child."

# 2

Images began racing through my mind again. I was transported into a scene from my childhood. I was twelve years old. My uncle came to visit us over the summer. I hadn't seen him in several years. Bill and I watched my young self looking back and forth from my dad to my uncle as each one spoke—a look of entertainment and wonder on my young face. I explained the background to Bill.

For years my dad had been my hero. I wanted to be just like him. And here was my uncle. He looked like my dad, but he was so different! My uncle ate moderately, exercised daily, and was fit and trim. My dad never exercised, ate as he pleased, and had developed diabetes and high blood pressure. My uncle enjoyed socializing but limited himself so he could spend more time with family and close friends. My dad's socializing knew no bounds. Sometimes one of his friends would call during dinner. He'd jump up, 'I've got to go!' grab his shoes and race out the door.

He and my uncle had once been business partners. My uncle would open the shop and stay past closing. My dad would open the shop, leave employees to run things while he hung out with friends, and only return in time to close. On one occasion I was with my uncle and we ran into one of my dad's business associates. He asked for my uncle's advice about a business idea. My uncle was honest with him—brutally honest! His lack of diplomacy shocked me. I asked him about it later. I'd seen that same guy come around and ask my dad for advice about the same idea, and my dad had spent a lot of time talking to him. Why had my uncle approached it differently? 'Look,' he said, 'your dad wants to be liked, so he tells that guy what he wants to hear. I'm telling him what he needs to hear.'

"This summer visit from my uncle is when I first started wondering about how to live," I said. "The contrast between him and my dad showed me there are different ways of approaching life—different ways of approaching conversation, or business, or health, or family. I think sometimes when kids see contrasting ways of life, they instinctively pick sides, loving one way and hating the other. But these were both men I loved and admired. Each had chosen to live one way instead of another. But why? What were their reasons?

"And that got me thinking: if there are different ways of living, are some better or worse than others? I started realizing that how I approached life was a matter of choice—my choice. I could choose how to live. In fact, I had to choose. There was no avoiding the choice. I had no choice but to choose. But how should I choose? How did people in general go about choosing how to live? I asked my father about it."

"What did he say?" Bill said.

"He said, 'Do good to other people. Have a lot of friends, have a family, and do good to them.'"

"Did he say what he meant by 'do good'?"

"I asked him. He just shrugged. So I tried answering my questions for myself. I started observing people around me, seeing how my friends, their parents, and even strangers approached life. Sometimes I'd ask questions about their approach. Often they seemed unaware of even having an approach: 'Doesn't everybody just… live?' Other times they gave me answers that puzzled me. Some scolded me for even asking: 'Just obey the elders!' You hear that a lot growing up in India: whatever your parents and the elders say is correct. There's little tolerance for questioning authority, and I could tell that most of the kids around me thought accepting authority without question was just the normal thing to do.

"It's funny: when I moved to the United States a few years later, I encountered the same attitude. The list of accepted authorities was different, but the willingness to accept whatever they said without question was the same. That wasn't for me. I had questions. I wanted answers. And I wanted those answers to be supported by reasons. I wanted to understand for myself what the reasons were—why one way of living was better than another. Whenever I read a book, watched a movie, listened to songs, or interacted with other people, I'd always be on the lookout for something that would give me insight about how best to live."

"What are some examples?" Bill said.

"One of the first sources I consulted was a book of famous quotes and wise sayings. But it disappointed me. There'd be a quote, and maybe it would express an interesting idea, but there'd be nothing supporting that idea—no study, no argument, no anecdote—no reasons at all for thinking the idea was true. It was the same with many people I met. They were committed to a way of living—to defending it, sharing it, raising their children in it—without having any clear reason why. Maybe somebody else had clear reasons for it (their parents, the elders—somebody), but they themselves didn't. It was as if they'd outsourced the most important decision in their life—the decision how to live—to someone else. They were just following a crowd."

"But following a crowd wasn't for you?" Bill said.

"Well… I wouldn't say that exactly," I said. "I did my share of following crowds too—especially in my late teens and early twenties."

The scene shifted again. I was transported to a time when I was a young adult. Bill and I watched my younger self on a Thursday afternoon. One text message after another began buzzing my phone—friends inviting me out for drinks. We watched together as I went out late that night with them, woke up hung over the next morning, and repeated the process the next night. And the next. And the next.

"It's a familiar pattern for a lot of people at this stage of life," Bill said. "What do you think of it now?"

"It was fun for a while," I said. "But it started wearing me down. Physically, I mean. Also emotionally."

"Why was that?" Bill said.

"I suppose it felt kind of… pointless? I couldn't see any purpose in what I was doing. It felt like I was just plodding forward in no meaningful direction."

Bill chuckled, then said in a deep, dramatic voice, "Tomorrow, and tomorrow, and tomorrow."

"What's that?" I said.

"A soliloquy from *Macbeth*:

> Tomorrow, and tomorrow, and tomorrow,
> Creeps in this petty pace from day to day,
> To the last syllable of recorded time;
> And all our yesterdays have lighted fools
> The way to dusty death. Out, out, brief candle!
> Life's but a walking shadow, a poor player,
> That struts and frets his hour upon the stage,
> And then is heard no more. It is a tale
> Told by an idiot, full of sound and fury,
> Signifying nothing.

"Macbeth reaches a point at which his entire life feels like a pointless plod—step after weary step to the grave, the only end he can clearly see."

"That sounds about right," I said. "I had Macbeth's problem: going from night to weary night with no clear purpose. I might have changed course sooner, but the relentless pace of partying kept me moving."

"So what ended up happening?"

"Humiliation halted me! I was traveling with some buddies in Peru and met an American girl at a club. We took a cab back to her apartment. I remember the smell of cat urine heavy in the air. But I didn't care. We started making out, cats weaving in and out between our feet. Without warning she shoved me: 'I want you to leave!' I was shocked: 'Right now?' 'Yes!' she said, 'Right now! Go!' I grabbed my phone and wallet and stumbled down the stairs to the street. I had no idea what had just happened. I also had no idea where I was. I hadn't noticed which direction the cab had taken us. My phone was dead. I had no local currency. I didn't speak the language, and I couldn't remember the name of my hotel. I climbed aboard a local bus headed in what I hoped was the right direction. It was about five o'clock in the morning. People on the bus were headed to work wearing hard hats or hospital scrubs. I was hunched in the back wearing my clubbing clothes and shame: '*What the fuck am I doing!?!*'" I paused. "Would Aristotle have anything to say about that?"

"About being a dumbass?"

"No!" I laughed. "About this stage in my life."

"Well yeah," Bill said. "I mean look: a lot of people aim for a life of sensory enjoyment—a life filled with things that please the senses, especially sex and intoxicants like alcohol. Aristotle says they're not crazy for thinking that's what it means to live well. We're biological beings, so we're hardwired to take pleasure in things like sex. In addition, when we look around, we see a lot of rich and famous people pursuing lives devoted to sensory enjoyment, and that gives some people the idea that that's how you're supposed to live. The problem, says Aristotle, is that a life devoted to sensory enjoyment is a life suited to grazing animals."

I laughed. "So people who live like that are like pigs—or cows or something like that?"

"Actually no," said Bill, "that's not what he means. You might be tempted to think that—as if he's criticizing people's taste, calling them vulgar or uncouth. But that isn't his point. His point is instead about the nature of pleasure. Pleasure or enjoyment is a byproduct of activity. It's the feeling that accompanies doing an activity well. Different activities give us different kinds of enjoyment. The enjoyment we get from using our taste buds is different from the enjoyment we get from using our eyes or ears. And the enjoyment we get from using our senses in general is different from the enjoyment we get from using a skill like shooting free throws or playing the piano.

"Grazing animals have a more limited range of abilities than humans have. Their lives don't include much beyond activities that stimulate the senses. So for them, living well doesn't involve much beyond sensory stimulation and the enjoyment that accompanies it. If we were grazing animals, the same would be true of us. But we're not grazing animals. For animals like us who are social and rational, there's more to life than the senses. So for animals like us, there's more to living well than stimulating the senses.

"You can devote yourself to chasing sensory enjoyment the way you and your young friends did. The problem is that it gets old. You outgrow it the same way you outgrow other activities. Think of a young child who learns a simple game like tic-tac-toe. It's fun at first. But the fun doesn't last. Once the child masters the game, boredom sets in, and the child starts looking for something new. The same happens with a life devoted to sensory enjoyment. It might be fun at first, but humans need more than sensory stimulation to flourish. After a while, boredom sets in, and they start craving something new. If they don't know any better, they might just seek out a different form of sensory enjoyment. But eventually the result is the same: boredom and desire for something new. That's true even when people are functioning in a psychologically healthy way.

I'm not even talking about cases in which they're using sensory enjoyment to distract themselves from some type of psychological pain."

"So what's the solution?" I said. "How do you break free of the enjoyment–boredom–novelty cycle?"

"The short answer is that you have to seek enjoyment in other kinds of activities, not sensory stimulation, but activities that develop and use a broader range of human abilities—like a child who drops tic-tac-toe and learns chess. If you don't expand your range of activities, you end up like a child who keeps playing tic-tac-toe past the point of boredom. The activities you engage in become less and less enjoyable, and if your life is largely devoted to those activities, you start enjoying your life less and less."

"So the idea is to avoid sensory enjoyment?" I said.

"No," Bill said. "Aristotle isn't opposed to sensory enjoyment. The enjoyment that accompanies sensory stimulation is part of human life. Aristotle isn't opposed to that any more than he's opposed to being human. His point is that sensory stimulation is only a part of human life. It can't be the whole because we're not grazing animals. For us to live well, we need to incorporate sensory enjoyment into our lives in a way that promotes overall well-being instead of preventing it.

"You and your young friends hadn't yet found a way of doing that, and you began experiencing the corrosive effects on your well-being. It's a common experience at that stage of life—the stage at which people start discovering their autonomy, their ability to make their own decisions and choose things they want instead of things other people want for them. But part of learning about autonomy is learning that you can exercise it for good or ill.

"You're perfectly free to choose this or that. But you aren't perfectly free to do well. Success in any domain depends on things besides your choice. A baseball pitcher is perfectly free to throw the ball wherever he wants, but he isn't perfectly free to throw a strike. To do that, he has to throw the ball within a particular zone. A violinist is perfectly free to make the violin produce all sorts of sounds, but she isn't perfectly free to make sounds that harmonize with the rest of the orchestra. To do that, she has to make sounds of specific frequencies. Investors are perfectly free to buy whatever stocks they want, but they aren't perfectly free to make money. To do that, they have to buy stocks that increase in value.

"It's the same with life as a whole. Think of a simple living thing like a plant. There are certain things it needs to thrive: the right kind of soil (neither too acidic nor too alkaline), the right amount of water (neither too much nor too little), the right amount of sunlight (neither too shady nor too direct). If the plant doesn't have these things, it won't live well. It might survive, but it won't flourish or thrive. Now imagine the plant could think, and imagine it said to itself, '*I don't need acidic soil. I don't need sunlight. I don't need water.*' It would be wrong. It would have false beliefs about what a biological being of its kind needs to flourish. And if it weren't anchored in the soil but were free to move around and pursue things it wanted, we might see it acting in ways that undermined its own well-being—spurning the right kind of soil or avoiding the right amount of sunlight or water.

"Humans are like that imaginary plant. They're biological beings who are perfectly free to think and act in all sorts of ways—including ways that undermine their own well-being. They're perfectly free to fail. They're perfectly free to ruin their lives and make themselves unhappy. What they aren't perfectly free to do is live well. To live well, they need to exercise their autonomy in specific ways. Not just any choices will do. They have to make the right kinds of choices—ones that actually promote well-being. There are conditions for living well, just as there are conditions for performing other activities well. It's not enough simply to believe you're doing what it takes to live well because your beliefs about well-being can be false. We see the results all around us: the world is full of unhappy people. None of them wants to be unhappy. They've nevertheless made themselves unhappy through choices they've freely made. If you're in that situation, hopefully you start getting a sense that you're on the wrong path the way you did. What happened after you became disenchanted with relentless partying?"

# 3

The scene shifted again. My younger self was driving to work in heavy traffic. It seemed like Bill and I were sitting in the back seat watching the scene unfold. "What's going on here?" Bill said.

I explained the background. "I decided to straighten out my life," I said. "No more partying! '*From now on,*' I thought, '*I'm going to do something worthwhile—something really meaningful. I'm going to make money!*' I started working at a bank and quickly moved into a management position. It was thrilling at first. Sometimes I'd earn more in a day than some people earned in a year. I'd feel happy and optimistic—like I was winning the game of life. But the feeling never lasted. A few days later, I'd be back to my normal self, hustling to make more. And more and more I surrounded myself with people who were also driven to make more. We called each other friends, but we always felt like competitors—each trying to outdo the others with job titles and conspicuous signals of success: cars, clothing, vacations, homes.

"After a couple years, I began feeling as if I'd somehow been cheated—as if someone had promised me that walking down this path would take me to a place where my life would have meaning or purpose, but instead the so-called path was just a treadmill. I was always striding forward, but never going anywhere—always reaching for the next big check or next big trophy. '"*But why?!*' I thought. '*Why does it matter whether I have a more expensive car than my friends, or a loftier job title, or a bigger house?*' What were all my efforts accomplishing in the end? I was wasting my talent chasing meaningless goals—ones I hadn't even chosen for myself. And it wasn't just my talent. I was wasting my life. There's only so much time, and I was spending all of mine doing… what? Accomplishing… what?"

Once again Bill said in a deep, dramatic voice, "Tomorrow, and tomorrow, and tomorrow."

"You mean… what you're saying is… I was repeating the same pattern? I had Macbeth's problem again, just this time with money?"

"Sounds like it, yes," Bill said. "I think I understand the background now. But how does that bring us to this scene in your car?"

"This day when I was driving to work, a thought crossed my mind: '*If I get into a wreck and am confined to a hospital bed, I'll feel happier than I feel going into the office.*'" Bill and I watched as my younger self got to work, walked into my manager's office, and submitted my notice. 'Take a walk with me,' my manager said. We went for a walk, his arm across my shoulders. 'What do you want?' he said. 'More money? A different position? Just tell me what you want.'

"The thing is," I said to Bill, "what I really wanted he couldn't give me."

"What was that?"

"A different kind of life. Money and titles weren't enough." I paused. "Did Aristotle have anything to say about money?"

"He did," Bill said. "He's actually one of the first people to talk about the functions of money. But when it comes to your question about how to live, his most important observation is that money is just a means to an end. The bills or coins or digits in your bank account aren't worth much to you by themselves. They have value only because you can use them to get other things you want. If all the things you wanted were free for the taking, you'd have no use for money. And if the only things you wanted were things money couldn't buy, you'd have no use for money."

"So is money a bad thing?"

"Not at all," Bill said. "Aristotle isn't saying money is bad. He's saying money is a tool. It's not good or bad in itself. Like any tool, its value derives from its use. So if someone is really dedicated to making more and more money, the way you were, we have to ask why: What are they using it for? What things do they think money will get them? It sounds like you were looking for money to get you two things: first, the admiration (or envy) of your friends, and second, some sense of meaning or purpose for your life. Money can help with the first aim, but it's unhelpful with the second for the reason I just mentioned: it's just a means to an end. It doesn't have value in itself. Its value derives entirely from what it can get you. Money can supply your life with meaning or purpose only if it gets you things that supply your life with meaning or purpose. In your case, it sounds like money was getting you the admiration of your friends. But the problem with admiration is that it isn't sufficient for overall well-being. So even if you get the admiration you want, you might still feel like something is missing."

"Can you say more about that?" I said.

"It'll help to see how admiration is woven into the broader fabric of human life—to understand why people want to be admired. If you look around at the living world, it's loaded with plants and animals that don't give a shit about admiration. So why do humans? The short answer is that we're social animals. Primate species like ours evolved to live in groups because there are advantages to group living: more eyes and ears to detect threats and opportunities in the environment, more hands and feet to collect food or chase down prey, and more access to potential mates. But there are also disadvantages to group living: more competition for scarce resources and potential mates. Evolution's strategy for balancing the advantages and disadvantages of group living is to have hierarchies within groups: some members of a group get priority access to things. They're higher up in the group's hierarchy.

"Animals like us want to secure positions higher up a group's hierarchy, and things that indicate a high position tend to make us feel good. That includes things like other people's admiration, respect, honor, or even envy. On the flipside, things that indicate a low position tend to make us feel bad—as if our well-being is threatened. Think of what we call 'ego.' It's a reflection of social hierarchy. People who have an ego often hate correction, hate admitting they're wrong, and envy people who are competent. They perceive both their own mistakes and other people's accomplishments as threats to their social position. On some level, they fear that if their mistakes are exposed or if other people are better than they are, they'll no longer have priority access to the things they need and want. So the human desire for admiration—or honor, fame, celebrity, whatever you want to call it—is a byproduct of being a social animal."

"Wait," I said, "it sounds like you're saying that humans can't help wanting admiration. So if it's a bad thing—"

"Wanting admiration isn't necessarily a bad thing," Bill said. "The problem is that admiration doesn't give you what you need to live well. For one thing, admiration depends more on what other people feel like admiring than it does on you and your abilities or accomplishments.

People don't have to admire you for anything you've done or anything you can do. They don't have to admire you for anything you care about, or for anything that contributes to living well. You can live well without admiration, and you can live badly with it."

"You've mentioned this idea of living well a couple times," I said. "Can you say more about it?"

"Sure," said Bill. "For Aristotle, living well is like doing well in any activity. Think of playing a sport. To play a sport well is a matter of developing and using the right kinds of abilities. According to Aristotle, the same is true of living well."

"I don't get it," I said. "How is living life like playing a sport?"

"Both are complex activities," Bill said. "Let's start with a sport. You play basketball, so let's think of what's involved in that. There's dribbling, running, jumping, shooting, passing, and so on. These are all activities. Combine these activities in the right way, in the right context—on the court with a hoop and some other players—and they compose a more complex activity: playing basketball. So playing basketball is a more complex, more encompassing activity that includes these other activities. The same is true of other sports. Each includes a range of activities that together compose the more encompassing activity that we call playing the sport."

"Okay," I said. "I get that, but I still don't get how that applies to life."

"If you think about living, it too is a complex activity. Think about what you do on a daily basis: eat, sleep, shower, walk, talk, shoot hoops, read, write, watch videos, listen to music. All of these are activities. Put them all together, and they compose a more complex activity that we call living. Now I'm simplifying things a bit. I've only mentioned the kinds of activities that might come to mind if someone said, 'Hey, Vishal, what did you do today?' But there are other activities we engage in on a daily basis that we tend not to think about, or that we might not even know about."

"What do you mean?" I said.

"I mean things like digesting food, or synthesizing proteins, or metabolizing sugars or fats. These are also things you do—activities you engage in that maintain your organs, tissues, and cells. They might not be top of mind when you think of things you do, but that doesn't mean they aren't important. In fact, they're essential. You can stop walking, talking, and shooting hoops, but you can't stop maintaining your organs, tissues, and cells. When a living thing stops performing those activities, it stops existing. It's dead.

"Now think of all the activities we've mentioned—everything from the metabolic activities that maintain your organs, tissues, and cells, to the ordinary activities that come to mind when someone asks what you did today. All of them together compose a more complex, more encompassing activity that we call living. So living is a complex activity like a sport. It encompasses a range of activities that together compose it. Living is more encompassing than playing a sport—that's true. You engage in many activities that aren't part of playing a sport, and you don't engage in any activities that aren't part of living your life. But living and playing a sport are still both complex activities. And the similarity between living and complex activities like sports enables Aristotle to gain insights about life using the patterns of reasoning we use to think about activities like sports."

"That's a lot to digest," I said.

"Do you want to take a break and talk about something else?"

"No, let's keep going. I still want to hear how all this applies to what we were talking about a minute ago: what Aristotle has to say about getting other people to admire you. You said that you can live well without admiration, and you can live badly with it."

"Right," said Bill, "we're almost there. Here's the next step: when you engage in an activity, you're using an ability you have. For example, when you dribble a basketball, you're using your ability to dribble a basketball—that's something you can do, and when you actually do it, you're using that ability. And the same is true for any other activity you engage in. To engage in that activity is to use an ability you have—the ability to engage in that very activity. Is that clear?"

"Yes," I said, "I think so. It seems like a really obvious point."

"It is," Bill said, "but it leads to some points that might be less obvious, so I want to make sure we go slowly. So let's look at all the abilities you have. You'll notice that some of them are like your ability to eat or sleep, or to experience emotions, or see or hear things, or move your limbs. These are abilities that didn't require training. You simply acquired them in the natural course of human development. They're abilities everyone acquires if nothing interferes with their development. Let's give abilities like these a name. Let's call them 'innate abilities.' Not all abilities are innate. Some abilities you don't just get. You instead have to work to acquire them through training, or practice, or repetition. Skills are an example. People aren't born knowing how to read or write, or play the violin, or dribble a basketball, nor do they just get these abilities in the natural course of their development. They instead have to acquire these abilities by repeatedly thinking, feeling, or acting in specific ways. Let's call abilities like these 'trained abilities.' Make sense so far?"

"Yes," I said.

"Ok, good. Let's focus on these trained abilities. We'll start with skills. If you think of the skills you have, you'll notice that some have a wider scope of application than others. A skill like, say, knowing how to throw a curveball has a very narrow scope of application. It enables you to achieve goals only within a very narrow domain. By contrast, skills like knowing how to read, or write, or think critically enable you to achieve goals in a much wider range of domains. Still with me?"

"I think so," I said. "You mean that being able to throw a curveball is useful if you're pitching in a baseball game, but it isn't much use beyond that, whereas critical thinking skills are useful in business, in sports, in politics, and in a wide range of other situations?"

"Exactly," Bill said. "Skills have different scopes of application. Some skills are more general—they have wider scopes of application. Other skills are more specific—they have narrower scopes of application. Now, Aristotle says there's another kind of trained ability. It's similar to a skill insofar as you acquire it through training, but it's different because its scope of application is even wider than the most general skills. Aristotle calls abilities like these excellences or virtues."

"What's an example?"

"Think of the ability to manage hardship—what people sometimes call 'fortitude.' Everyone faces hardship. I don't mean just the hardship that results from some type of bad event or situation. I mean even the hardship you face when confronting daily challenges like learning something new. When you start learning something new—like how to golf, say—you fail a lot more than you succeed. The number of bad swings you make far exceeds the number of good ones. It takes ongoing correction and repetition to train yourself to swing the club the right way. That process of correction and repetition can be uncomfortable physically and emotionally. If you don't have the ability to push through that discomfort—to confront the hardship and do what you have to do despite it—you're not going to learn the new skill. And it's not just that skill you'll have trouble learning, it's any skill: mathematics or writing, singing or dancing, playing the piano or violin, parenting or managing long-term loving relationships—you'll have trouble learning and getting better at any of these skills if you can't manage hardship well.

"So the ability to manage hardship is necessary for acquiring skills. If you can't manage hardship—if you don't have that virtue—your ability to acquire skills will be compromised. But the ability to manage hardship is even more general than that. Hardship is so pervasive in human life, it's hard to imagine any aspect of your life that won't be compromised if you can't manage hardship well—your work, your relationships with other people, your ability to bounce back from mistakes or bad luck. On the flip side, it's hard to imagine any aspect of your life that won't benefit if you can manage hardship well. So the ability to manage hardship is so general that it improves almost every dimension of human life, and its absence compromises almost every dimension of human life. Trained abilities with that kind of generality are what Aristotle calls virtues. And what's important about virtues is that having them enables you to live well. They're analogous to the abilities that enable you to play a sport well except that the activity they enable you perform well isn't a sport, it's life."

"I was following you up to that last point," I said. "Can you say more?"

"Think again of the analogy with playing a sport," Bill said. "To play a sport well is a matter of acquiring and using the right kinds of abilities. If you have and use those abilities, you'll play the sport well. And if you don't have those abilities or don't use them, you won't play well."

"Okay, I got that."

"All right. Now, in the case of a sport, the abilities that enable you to perform well are skills. But suppose the abilities we're talking about aren't skills. Suppose they're much more general than that. Suppose they're virtues—those very general abilities like the ability to manage hardship well, or to manage emotion well, or friendship well, or decision-making well—abilities that touch almost every aspect of human life. Just as having and using the right skills enables you to play a sport well, having and using those abilities—the virtues—enables you to do something well. But what the virtues enable you to do well is live.

Virtues are so general in their scope that the activity they enable you to perform well is the complex all-encompassing activity that we call living. So for Aristotle, to live well is to acquire and use the virtues, just as to play a sport well is to acquire and use the right kinds of skills."

I was struggling to assemble all the ideas Bill had just explained. I tried rehearsing them back to him: "So… the analogy with skills and sports… having and using skills enables you to play a sport well… Aristotle says that having and using the virtues enables you to live well… and… the connection between living life and playing a sport… they're both complex activities?"

"That's right," said Bill. "And since they're both complex activities, Aristotle uses the same concepts to think about living that we use to think about complex activities that are more familiar—the activities that we tend to think of when someone asks us what we did today."

"But… I still don't see how this helps to understand the point about other people's admiration," I said.

"Okay," said Bill. "Let's get to that. The main idea is that you can live well without admiration, and you can live badly with it. The points I just rehearsed for you explain why. Performing an activity well is a matter of getting and using the right kinds of abilities. Whether you have and use those abilities doesn't depend on what other people think or feel about you. It doesn't depend on other people's admiration. If you have those abilities, you have them independent of whether anyone recognizes or admires you for them. And if you lack those abilities, other people's admiration isn't going to magically give them to you.

"What's true of any complex activity is true of life. Living well is a matter of getting and using the right kinds of abilities—the virtues. Whether you have and use the virtues doesn't depend on other people's admiration. If you have the virtues, you have them independent of whether anyone admires you, and their admiration isn't going to magically make you virtuous. You acquire the virtues by training, practice, and repetition—the same way you acquire any trained ability—not by someone applauding you.

"And Aristotle makes a further point: what people feel like admiring one day might change the next. But that's not true of an ability you've acquired through training and practice. If you've trained yourself to manage hardship—if you've practiced managing it well and done it again and again and again—it's practically impossible for you to think, feel, or act any other way. That ability becomes part of who you are. An ability like that can't just change overnight the way people's admiration can. That's why fame is fickle, but living well is lasting: living well depends on having and using trained abilities.

"Suppose, then, that you want to live well, but you're channeling all your efforts toward securing other people's admiration. The results will be similar to what you experienced when you were chasing sensory enjoyment. When people admire you for something, it'll feel good. But that feeling will soon wear off, and you'll go in search of something new. You'll look for someone new to admire you, or something new for them to admire you for. And the cycle will repeat itself. The only way to break free of that cycle is to channel your efforts differently: not toward securing other people's admiration, but toward securing excellence—especially excellence in managing the inescapable dimensions of human life: hardship, failure, emotion, interpersonal relationships, sensory enjoyment, knowledge, time, decision-making, and so on.

"These aren't excellences specific to one activity. They're general human excellences—abilities that enable humans to engage well in the activity of living. Trying to live life without them is like trying to play a sport without the skills. It doesn't matter how much money you have or how many fans. Those things aren't going to give you the abilities you need. It's the same with life as a whole."

"So will money and fans prevent you from living well?" I said.

"Not necessarily. Aristotle isn't saying that money and fans are bad. He's instead saying that money and fans are limited goods. Neither is sufficient for living well. You have to see each for the kind of good it is. You have to understand what it can contribute to human well-being and what it can't, and then pursue it in a way that reflects its real value."

# 4

"So my mistake wasn't that I wanted to make money?" I said. "My mistake was instead thinking that money was going to give me everything I wanted in life?"

"That's one way to put it," Bill said. "Another is to say that money is just a means to an end. If you know that's the kind of thing money is, then a decision to make money assumes you've already determined what you want money for."

"What if you don't know what you want money for? Is there any harm in just having it?" I said.

"Not necessarily," Bill said. "Again, Aristotle doesn't say money is a bad thing. He says it's a tool. So think of the way you'd think of any other tool. Suppose I said to you, 'Vishal, I really want a rotary hammer!' And you said, 'What do you want it for?' And I said, 'No reason. I just want it. Is there any harm in just having it?' At that point, you might say, 'Well, there's no harm in just having it, I suppose. But isn't it a little silly to want a tool even though there's nothing you plan on doing with it?' You might even go a step further and say, 'There's no harm in having the tool itself, but there might be harm in forgoing other things in order to get it. What's the opportunity cost? Aren't there better ways of using your resources than getting a tool you don't want for any particular job?' We could apply a similar line of reasoning to your decision to make money. You realized it was costing you both your time and your talent, and you realized a life devoted to money-making wasn't worth that sacrifice. At some level, you were asking yourself more basic life questions, and your answers to those questions didn't match the way you were living."

"What do you mean 'basic life questions'?"

"I mean questions like 'What activities am I going to engage in?' and 'What abilities am I going to acquire?' Remember, life is composed of nothing but activities. Your life ends up being composed of whatever activities you choose to engage in. And to engage in each of those activities is to use some ability you have. So if we ask, 'How are you going to live your life?' that question reduces to 'What activities are you going to engage in?' and 'What abilities are you going to cultivate?'

"Now consider your life as a whole—from start to finish, all eighty or ninety years you expect to live. View that life as if it's a chunk of raw material—something you can sculpt like a piece of marble. Except you don't sculpt it with a hammer and chisel. You sculpt it instead with the choices you make: how you choose to respond to anger or other emotions, how you choose to make decisions, how you choose to indulge in sensory enjoyments, how you choose to manage friendships, how you choose to manage hardships, mistakes, and failures.

"These choices aren't isolated episodes. Over time, they become stable patterns of thinking, feeling, and acting. If you act impulsively on anger once, you're more likely to act impulsively on anger in the future. And if you continue acting impulsively on anger, you eventually just become someone who manages anger badly—someone with an anger management problem, as we say. That impulsive pattern of thinking, feeling, and acting becomes part of the shape of your life—part of what you've sculpted with the choices you've made.

"On Aristotle's view, then, asking 'How should I live my life?' is like asking 'How should I shape the life I've been given?' And answering that question requires you to ask what kinds of activities you want your life to comprise: 'What activities am I going to engage in?' and 'What abilities am I going to cultivate?' It sounds like at some level you were asking yourself these questions. You realized there was a disparity between the activities you were engaging in on a daily basis, and the activities you would choose to engage in all things considered. That brings us back to your story. What happened after you left the bank?"

Images began racing through my mind again. I was transported to a scene in which I was talking with my mother in Punjabi. "What's she saying to you?" Bill said.

"She's asking me if I'm going to become a monk."

Bill laughed. "Okay, tell me how we got here."

"I left the bank because I wanted to do something different with my life—something I really wanted to do, not something scripted by other people to achieve some end they had chosen. The problem was that I didn't really know what I wanted to do. Around this time I had a conversation with one of my uncles—my mother's brother. 'Gandhi is my hero,' he said, 'I follow what he does.' So I got a copy of Gandhi's book, *The Story of My Experiments with Truth*, and tried living the way Gandhi did. Gandhi practiced brahmacharya—a rigorous form of asceticism: no sex, no alcohol or other intoxicants, no movies or music, a strict diet, regular fasting, a simple bed. Before I had been following crowds and indulging my appetites. Now I was doing exactly the opposite—abstaining from all forms of enjoyment in order to gain control over myself. And it worked! I loved that aspect of it. I loved the discipline and self-control I was developing."

"So what was the problem?" Bill said.

"The problem was… I wasn't really enjoying life. I liked being around other people. I enjoyed sharing food and drink, and conversation and entertainment. Now I was turning away from all that in an effort to become independent and self-reliant. But in fact, I was just becoming isolated and lonely. After a year, it started taking a toll. My mother was the first to notice. She saw me turning away from social gatherings and interactions with friends and family. She was worried, I suppose. That's when we had this conversation—when she's asking me if I plan on becoming a monk. Would Aristotle have anything to say about this stage in my life?"

"He would," Bill said. "We can start by noting the difference between self-discipline and self-denial. Self-discipline is about training your desires and emotions—learning to control them so they don't control you. Self-denial, by contrast, is about pretending you don't have desires and emotions. It's one thing to discipline your desire for food or drink or sex so you pursue them at the right time, in the right way, for the right reasons, and to the right extent. It's another to pretend you don't have those biological drives.

"The difference between self-discipline and self-denial corresponds to the difference we discussed earlier between Aristotelians and Stoics. Aristotelians promote self-discipline—training your desires and emotions, harnessing and directing them so they promote human well-being instead of preventing it. But Stoics go beyond that aspiration. We saw earlier that Seneca and Cicero aim not at training desires and emotions but at eliminating them. And the same is true of many Buddhists and ascetics like Gandhi.

"Emotions and desires are powerful in human life because we're biological beings. For that reason we need to train them and carefully monitor their influence on us so they don't have a destructive effect on the fabric of our lives. But that's different from trying to eliminate them. Think of it this way: imagine you're running a zoo with wild animals. You need to ensure they're healthy and well maintained, but you also need to ensure they're well contained. Some are dangerous if left to themselves. You can't just let them roam free. You need to keep them within bounds. But that's different from starving or mistreating them. You need to nourish and care for them and give them scope to be what they are.

"Aristotelians treat desires and emotions the way you'd treat the dangerous animals in the zoo. You need to give your desires and emotions a limited scope of operation that's carefully circumscribed and designed to contribute to living well. But you can't neglect them or eliminate them. That's an unrealistic—and undesirable—goal. We're emotional animals. You can't change that. To pretend otherwise is exactly that: pretending. And it's a kind of pretending that leads to difficulties if put into practice—like the difficulty you had coping with your father's death. What you liked about Gandhi's brahmacharya was that it helped you learn self-discipline. What you didn't like is that it took you toward self-denial. It had you thinking that you needed to deny your desire for social interaction. But that desire is rooted in human biology. We're social animals, just as we're emotional animals. You can't deny one any more than you can deny the other. If you try, you end up feeling alienated from yourself—like a stranger in your own skin."

"That's a good way of describing it," I said. "I felt like a stranger in my own skin—as if I was trying to live someone else's life. Listen, I want to go back to something you said earlier."

"Okay," Bill said.

"You were talking about virtues. I remember reading somewhere that Aristotle had this idea that a virtue was a mean between two extremes: not doing too much of something or too little of something, but the right amount. Is that right?"

"Kind of," said Bill. "Aristotle introduces the idea of a mean between extremes as a starting point for explaining what a virtue is. It's easiest to apply the idea to something like sensory enjoyment. You know from experience that there are better and worse ways of integrating sensory enjoyment into your life. Some are compatible with living well, others aren't. If you engage in sensory enjoyment too much—like you and your young party buddies did—then you become a glutton or drunkard. If you engage in it too little—like you did in your experiment with Gandhi's asceticism—you become engaged in unhealthy self-denial. So there are two extremes: an extreme of excess and an extreme of defect: too much sensory enjoyment on the one hand, and too little sensory enjoyment on the other. The right way of integrating sensory enjoyment into your life is between those two extremes—neither too much nor too little. That would be a way of engaging in sensory enjoyment that contributes to living well.

"The ability to engage in sensory enjoyment in the right way, at the right times, in the right manner, and for the right reasons—and to do that not just on occasion but consistently—that would be a virtue, the virtue of temperance (or moderation, self-discipline, self-control—whatever you want to call it). But the idea of a mean between extremes is just a starting point for understanding what a virtue is. It doesn't apply equally well to all the virtues Aristotle talks about, and even when it does apply to a virtue, it does so only in a limited way."

"So what's the clearer way of understanding a virtue?" I said.

"It's an ability with two components: first, the ability to judge accurately in particular situations what contributes to living well, and second, the ability to think, feel, and act in ways that line up with those judgments. Think again of the virtue of temperance—say, temperance regarding alcohol. If you're temperate, then you know in particular situations whether you should drink, and what, and how much. You might know that, say, having a beer after a stressful day at work will help you relax and be fully present for your family, but you know that having a beer before doing work on the roof of your house isn't a good idea. You might generally abstain from alcohol, but you know that you should make an exception to celebrate your friend's promotion. Moreover, you'll know that a couple shots will be fine, but that you should take your time and sip the third. If you're temperate, then you'll know in general how to use alcohol in ways that contribute to living well, and you'll judge accurately in particular situations how to use it in those ways.

"But temperance involves more than just knowing these things. You have to think, feel, and act in line with that knowledge. If you know that you should use alcohol in a certain way, but can't do it, or do it only with painful effort, then you don't have the virtue. Think again of an analogy with sports: if you know the right way to shoot, but can't shoot that way, you haven't yet mastered the ability. The same is true of a virtue. And because virtues are so general, they involve not just specific actions, but thoughts and feelings too. If you act the right way, but feel pain or resentment or fear, you don't have the virtue. Finally, because virtues are abilities, we're talking about ways of thinking, feeling, and acting that you perform consistently. If you use alcohol the right way on only one occasion and use it wrongly on many others, you don't have the virtue. Likewise, if you sink a three-pointer on only one occasion and miss on all the others, we don't say you're a good three-point shooter."

"So what's the right way to drink?" I said.

"A way that contributes to living well," Bill said.

"No, I mean like how much should you drink and when? I'm looking for specific details."

"There is no one-size-fits-all formula," Bill said. "The details depend on your specific circumstances. Think just of the amount: if you weigh eighty pounds, the right amount is going to be different than if you weigh two-hundred pounds. Likewise, the right amount is going to vary depending on what you plan on doing—if, for instance, you need to drive home or do something that requires manual dexterity. Similarly, if you're a recovering alcoholic, or if you've taken a lifelong vow to abstain from alcohol, the right amount is none. For you, temperance means abstaining completely. So there's no one-size-fits-all answer to your question. That's why virtues are abilities, not exceptionless rules.

"If there were rules for living well that applied to everyone in all circumstances, then living well would be easy: you'd just have to follow the rules. But Aristotle sees that life isn't like that—no complex activity is. There's no one-size-fits-all rule for being a great basketball player either. Being a great basketball player is instead a matter of learning and practicing abilities which you then use in particular situations. The same is true of any complex activity including living. The abilities you need to learn and practice in order to live well are virtues. To have a virtue—like the virtue of temperance—is to have an ability to judge accurately in particular circumstances what contributes to living well, and to think, feel, and act in line with that judgment. So if you're temperate, you'll judge accurately in particular situations whether to drink, and what to drink, and how much, and for what reasons. And you'll actually drink in that way—a way that contributes to living well—and you'll do it consistently.

"Let's get back to your story: What happened after your experiment with asceticism?"

# 5

The scene shifted again. I was transported to a workshop I'd attended a few years ago. Bill and I watched as a man sitting across from me grilled me on some responses I'd written on a form. "What's going on here?" Bill said.

"After the Gandhi thing," I said, "I pivoted again. I turned to self-help books in the hopes of finding better ideas about how to live. I started with the godfather of self-help—Benjamin Franklin—and progressed to books by other self-help gurus."

"What are some examples?"

"There are so many. Just off the top of my head, I'd say *The 7 Habits of Highly Effective People* by Stephen R. Covey, *Tools of Titans* and *The 4-Hour Workweek* by Timothy Ferriss, *A Guide to the Good Life* by William B. Irvine, *Steve Jobs* by Walter Isaacson, *The Seven Spiritual Laws of Success* by Deepak Chopra, *The Obstacle Is the Way* and *Ego Is the Enemy* by Ryan Holiday, *The Power of Now* by Eckhart Tolle, *Total Recall* by Arnold Schwarzenegger, *Siddhartha* by Hermann Hesse, *Awaken the Giants Within* by Tony Robbins, the *Tao Te Ching*, *Change Your Thoughts – Change*

*Your Life* by Wayne W. Dyer, *Self-Reliance* by Ralph Waldo Emerson… Is that enough to give you an idea of the kinds of things I was reading?"

"It is, thanks," said Bill. "What did you think of the books you read—or what do you think of them now?"

"Some had useful practical tips for optimizing routine tasks—like the Covey and Ferriss books. The problem is that they didn't have anything to say about how to live life. Others had ideas about it, but they were vague or unjustified—like the *Tao Te Ching* or the stuff by Chopra and Dyer. It was hard knowing how to put what they said into practice because it was so unclear. Also, they didn't really explain why you should do what they said. They just expected you to accept it—like an article of religious faith.

"Sometimes the books I read contradicted each other. For example, Chopra promoted a spontaneous, intuitive approach to life that was at odds with the more proactive, structured approach promoted by people like Covey. Similarly, the *Tao Te Ching* emphasized simplicity, humility, and living in harmony with the natural way or Tao. This was totally opposed to the ruthless, goal-oriented intensity promoted by people like Steve Jobs. Likewise, *Siddhartha* described a spiritual journey that renounced worldly desires in pursuit of personal enlightenment—something opposed to the worldly success promoted by many of the other books I read.

"Also, I wasn't really thinking critically about what I was reading. I focused less on what authors said and more on how they said it. I'd be impressed by clever turns of phrase—like Ben Franklin's 'Early to bed and early to rise' quote. They were pleasing to the ear, like clever hip-hop songs. That didn't make what they said true, or relevant, or useful. But back then (it was before you and I started working together), I didn't evaluate what the authors were saying in a critical way. I was just carried along by whatever sounded good. It's no surprise that a lot of authors who've done well in the self-help genre are good marketers who've found clever ways of packaging whatever they have to say. It took me a while to realize the wrapper was better than the contents inside.

"The more *New York Times* bestsellers I read, the more I got the impression that they followed a formula—the way pop songs do. When you first hear pop music, you're really into it because the music industry has a formula that it knows a lot of people like. They aren't looking to please people with sophisticated musical tastes because that's not most people. Most people are average listeners, so the industry targets the fat part of the musical-taste bell curve and delivers the kinds of sounds average listeners like to hear. But after a while, the songs start to sound more or less the same—the same rhythms, the same chord progressions, the same lyrical themes. The music gets predictable, and you get bored.

"It's the same with the legacy publishing industry. It's looking for mass distribution, so it doesn't target people with sophisticated literary tastes because that's not most people. It instead targets average readers, and it has a formula for giving them content they like to consume. The books I was reading started to feel the same as pop songs. They got predictable, I got bored, and when I got bored, I got more critical. I was no longer carried away by whatever sounded good and began focusing more on what authors were saying instead of just how they were saying it."

"What's an example of the predictability you're talking about?"

"You'd hear some version of the hero's journey over and over: here's a guy, here's an obstacle, he overcomes it. I get that the hero's journey is a way of telling a story that connects with a lot of readers, but if you read enough books like that, it starts getting old. It's like with pop music. You think, 'You're just playing A, D, and G chords the whole fucking time!' The other thing is, sometimes the hero they'd talk about—someone like Steve Jobs—wasn't really a good person, all things considered. He could treat other people really badly.

"I should mention: I didn't just read these books. I tried applying what they said to my life, just as I'd done with Gandhi. My self-help experiments culminated in a project I called Evolve 30. It was inspired by Tim Ferriss. I'd take an idea—intermittent fasting, cold showers, a fruit-only diet, waking every day at 5 a.m.—and try it for thirty days to see where it got me."

"What were your results?"

"In the end, nothing I tried got me very far. I learned some helpful tips and tricks, but nothing answered my fundamental question: How should I live my life? When I go back now and reread the books that impressed me, the ideas seem pretty shallow. The things I tried were almost all about optimizing means to ends. For example, if you want to be a great entrepreneur, do this; if you want to get better at free throws, do that; if you want to lose twelve pounds in a week, do this other thing. I have no problem optimizing means to ends. If someone suggests a better way of achieving an end I'm pursuing, that's fine. But I was always wondering about the ends themselves. Should I want to be a great entrepreneur? Should I want to get better at free throws? Should I want to lose twelve pounds in a week? Were any of these ends worth achieving? Were any of them worth whatever time and effort it'd take to achieve them? Were any of them worth having in life?

"The books I read didn't really say anything about which ends were worthwhile. Most simply assumed you wanted—or should want—the ends they were talking about. They didn't bother explaining why those ends, and not others, were worth your time and effort. There was no principle—no system—for evaluating them. But that's what I was looking for. I wanted to know how best to live. That meant evaluating not just different means of achieving goals, but evaluating goals themselves."

"So in general," Bill said, "the books you read would say, 'If you want to achieve X, then do Y,' but you were interested in whether achieving X was worthwhile in the first place?"

"That's right."

"So how does that bring us to this scene where this guy is grilling you?"

"I attended a workshop in Arizona that epitomized the means-focused approach to things. The organizers asked you to select goals from each of four categories: business, personal, relationship, and community. They'd then work with you on making those goals SMART: Specific, Measurable, Achievable, Relevant, and Time-bound. Other group members would then stress test your SMART goals by formulating objections to them. Finally, the organizers would help you formulate contingency plans in case things didn't go as expected. This scene we're watching is one of the organizers helping me transform one of my goals into a SMART goal. The workshop was a helpful exercise—especially for people who were used to inheriting goals from others instead of formulating goals for themselves. But what strikes me about the approach in retrospect is that there were no principles for choosing goals except whether you could make them SMART."

"Wait…" Bill said. "The only principle for selecting goals was whether it was possible to find some means of achieving them?"

"That's right," I said. "Don't get me wrong: it's good to have goals you can actually achieve. But I wanted more. I wanted goals that were actually worth achieving, and neither the workshop nor any of the self-help books I was reading had much to say about that. Their aim, it seemed, was to satisfy people's desire for agency—to show people that they could set goals for themselves and achieve them. That's not a bad thing. But I wanted more. I wanted a way of determining which goals I should choose instead of just choosing goals at random."

"What are some examples of the goals you set?" Bill said.

"I recall one of my goals was waking up at 6 a.m. every day for three weeks and running two miles. Another was taking my mom to dinner every week for ten weeks. I accomplished one goal, felt good about it, then moved on to the next goal. And the next goal. And the next." I paused. "I can see now… it was the same pattern as before: Macbeth's problem all over again. I think that, in retrospect, what I was looking for was some type of principle for evaluating goals—a tool to tell me whether a goal was worth my time and effort."

"That makes sense," Bill said. "If you don't know what goals are worth pursuing, you're likely to run into

Macbeth everywhere you turn. The difference you noticed between evaluating means to ends and evaluating ends themselves is how Aristotle distinguishes being wise from being merely clever."

# 6

"Wise versus clever?" I said.

"Wise versus merely clever," Bill said. "Wise people are clever, but not all clever people are wise."

"Can you explain?"

"Clever people are good at finding means to ends; they know how to get what they want. But the things they want might not be worth wanting. The ends they pursue might not contribute to living well. Wisdom requires more. Wise people are clever: they too know how to get what they want. But they also know which things are worth wanting. They know which ends contribute to living well, and which ends have priority over others."

"Sometimes you meet these people," I said, "I knew some at the bank—they're really smart, but you look at what they're using their intelligence for, and you think, '*What a waste of brain power!*' What would Aristotle say about them?"

"It sounds like they're clever fools," Bill said.

"Clever fools?"

"They have the brain power to find efficient means to ends, right?"

"Right."

"But you're saying the ends they're pursuing aren't worthwhile?"

"Correct."

"Wisdom doesn't pursue ends that aren't worthwhile—that don't contribute to overall well-being. So the people you're describing aren't wise, yet they're still really smart?"

"Yes."

"So these people are merely smart—merely clever. They have a lot of brain power, they could be using it for something worthwhile, but they're not. That's foolish. So they're clever yet foolish. They're clever fools. It sounds like a lot of the self-help books you were reading might belong in the same category: merely clever. They suggested better means of achieving this or that end. That's clever. But you wanted more. You wanted advice about the ends themselves. You wanted wisdom, and the books you were reading didn't give you that. Without some way of evaluating ends themselves, self-help books can make you really good at doing things that aren't worthwhile. You can learn the best ways of achieving all sorts of things that don't really matter in the grand scheme of human life."

"They'll turn you into a clever fool?" I said.

"They can," Bill said. "Whether or not they do depends on how you use them."

"So what do I have to do to become wise instead of merely clever?"

"Well for one thing, wisdom requires reflection."

"Can you explain?"

"We're rational animals," Bill said. "Part of being rational is trying to understand the meaning or purpose of things—including the meaning or purpose of our lives. We understand our lives in part by telling stories that explain who and what we are and what kind of place the world is. Crafting that kind of story requires patient reflection on yourself and your life circumstances: your past and present, your strengths and weaknesses, your successes and failures, your fears and ambitions, your loves and hates, friends and foes, mentors and pupils, your daily struggles and life-changing calamities—all of these things and more need to find a place within that story if you're going to make sense of your life. It's only in the context of that kind of story that you can develop an understanding of what really matters in life.

"Without a story that makes sense of your life, you run into Macbeth's problem. You experience the pain of pointlessness—the pain that animals like us feel when our lives don't seem to have a clear meaning or purpose. But you can't craft that kind of story if you never stop to reflect—if you're partying non-stop, or working non-stop, or reading non-stop, or jumping non-stop from one self-help experiment to another.

"Your self-help experiments had you choosing goals arbitrarily, simply to incentivize more activity. Likewise, your nonfiction addiction had you reading more and more. But what you needed wasn't to read more, but to read less and understand more. Relentless activity prevents reflection—including reflection on what really matters in life. Without reflection there's no way of situating goals and activities within a broader story about human well-being that explains why those goals and activities are worth pursuing. So there was nothing that enabled you to answer the question, 'How should I live my life?' or even, 'Why am I doing what I'm doing?' Yet being able to answer these questions is something you wanted—and something you needed in order to feel as though your life had meaning."

"Wait… you're saying that to find meaning in your life all you have to do is make up some story about yourself and your place in the universe?"

"It's not quite that simple," Bill said. "For one thing, not all stories are true. Sometimes we tell ourselves a story about our place in the universe, and the universe comes back and tells us that our story is false. When that happens it's disorienting."

"What do you mean?" I said.

"I mean when you've been telling yourself that the world is this kind of place and you fit into the world in this kind of way, and then it turns out that the world isn't that kind of place or you don't fit into it the way you thought, then the experience can be confusing and painful—confusing, because it no longer seems clear to you what kinds of things are worthwhile in life; and painful, because in your confusion you can experience a lot of emotions, and you don't know how to understand them."

"Can you give me some examples?"

"You can feel sadness, like you've lost something valuable. You can feel anger, like someone has taken something valuable from you. You can feel fear, like something bad is going to happen either to you or to the people or things you care about. And you can feel all these things together—all these emotions can well up inside you without warning—first one, then another, then another. And to make matters worse, you can't understand why you feel the ways you do."

"I'm not sure I get that last part," I said.

"Think again of your father's death. Losing something valuable, like someone you love, inspires grief. That's the natural human response to loss. If you know that, then you can understand why you feel the way you do. You know that you've lost something valuable, and that you're experiencing grief because of that loss. You can tell yourself, 'I've lost something. I need to allow myself to grieve.' And if you know how to manage emotions—if you have that virtue—then you'll manage your grieving well. But suppose you don't know these things. Suppose you don't realize you've lost something, or suppose you don't know that grief is the natural response to loss. In that case, you won't know why you feel the ways you do.

All you'll know is that you're in pain. And that inability to make sense of your own experience is itself painful. Does that make sense?"

"I think so," I said, "but what does that have to do with the thing you were talking about before—when the story you've been telling yourself about your place in the world turns out false?"

"Losing confidence in that story," Bill said, "is like losing anything else you value. If there's a difference, it's that people don't always realize they've lost something. Think, by contrast, of losing your father: it was obvious. He was here—a concrete, physical individual that you could see and hear and touch—and then he wasn't. But when we're talking about losing your self-understanding—losing confidence in the story you've been telling yourself about who you are and your place in the universe—the loss often isn't that obvious. People often don't know they've lost something they valued. The loss is something they feel—it causes them sadness, or anger, or fear. But the loss isn't something they think of as a loss. What they think is disconnected from how they feel, and that disconnect prevents them from understanding why they feel the ways they do. They can't say to themselves, 'I've lost something. I need to allow myself to grieve' because they don't think of their loss as a loss."

"What do they think of it as?"

"Often they don't think of it at all. All they know is they're in pain. Sometimes they respond to that pain by looking around for a cause, and often that search takes the form of blame: trying to find someone they can accuse of causing the pain they're experiencing." Bill paused. "Some dark chapters in human history have resulted from attempts to assign blame for misunderstood pain.

"But let's get back to your story. You've said you've been on a journey since childhood trying to gain insight about how to live. Journeys cross distances to reach a destination, and often travelers make wrong turns along the way. Your relentless partying, your fixation on money-making and admiration, your experiments with self-denial, self-help, and Stoicism: you've described all these as wrong turns on the road to your destination."

"Wait," I said. "What's my destination?"

"Based on what you've described, your destination is wisdom. That's where you've been wanting to get. You didn't use that term, but your description of the kind of thing you've been searching for matches the contours of wisdom—what Aristotle called *phronesis* in Greek. In fact, if I had to guess, I'd say the search for wisdom is also what got you here, to this conversation. Maybe you thought that taking psychedelics would magically give you insight about how to live—that they'd help you find wisdom?"

I laughed. "Maybe something like that, yes. But okay: suppose you're right, and I've been seeking wisdom this whole time. Go on."

"The overarching story you've been telling yourself about your place in the world depicts you as a traveler on a journey to wisdom. When you view your life from that perspective, the various wrong turns you've taken look simply like episodes in the ongoing journey to your destination. But you didn't have to take that perspective on your life. You could've been telling yourself a different story this whole time.

"Imagine, for instance, that instead of depicting yourself as a traveler you'd been depicting yourself as, say, a Stoic hero—a solitary individual carving his path through the world unphased by grievous losses and enduring the slings and arrows of outrageous fortune with complete equanimity. If you'd been committed to the Stoic story—if you'd really been convinced you were a Stoic hero—then your father's death might have left you without a clear sense of who you were. It would've shown you that you weren't impervious to pain and weren't built for isolation. But if not a Stoic hero, then what? And how to approach life, or love, or loss, or money, or health, or life at large if not as a Stoic—if that's not who you really are?

"Before, the Stoic story would've provided a model for approaching life. It would've told you which things were valuable and which weren't. But once you realized the story was false, it would no longer have been clear to you which things had real value—which things you should be pursuing in life and which not. If you'd really been convinced you were a Stoic hero, the falsification of that story would've left you without a sense of ultimate purpose in life. That's what I mean when I say that it's disorienting when your self-understanding gets falsified. Is that clear now?"

"I think so," I said.

"Now, in fact, you weren't committed to the Stoic story, so discovering its falsity wasn't devastating to you because you weren't really committed to seeing yourself as a Stoic hero. You were instead committed to seeing yourself as a traveler, and according to the traveler story, your encounter with Stoicism was just a wrong turn in an ongoing journey. And the same was true of your encounters with relentless partying, money-making, self-help, and the rest. The failure of each of these things to satisfy you wasn't devastating because you were viewing them from a wider perspective, and from that perspective each of them looked simply like a wrong turn—something from which you could turn away and correct course."

"So suppose," I said, "that you find out that the story you've been telling yourself about yourself is false, and you're disoriented in the way you describe. What do you do? How do you get over it?"

"The short answer," Bill said, "is that you come up with a new story that's closer to the truth."

"That's it?!"

"That's the short answer, yes. Finding meaning in life is an ongoing process of updating and revising the story we tell ourselves about ourselves and the universe we inhabit."

"What's the long answer?" I said.

"The long answer has to do with updating whatever self-understanding you have. I'd have to know more about you and your circumstances to give you a long answer."

"I'm not sure I understand," I said.

"Think of a sports analogy. You ask me how to improve your golf game, and I say, 'Well, the short answer is hit the ball in ways that take strokes off your game.' You say, 'Duh! I want details.' To give you those details, I'm going to need to know more about your game. Once I've seen how you use woods and irons, how you chip, and putt, and whatnot, then I can make more detailed suggestions about improving your game. Something analogous is true here."

"I've just told you a bunch of things about my life," I said, "and you seem to have some insight about it—the journey I've been on. Doesn't that give you enough information to suggest some next steps on my journey?"

"We've only been talking for about an hour," Bill said. "That doesn't make me an expert on your life. And keep in mind that I only know what you've told me, and your impressions about your life—the impressions we all have about our own lives—are incomplete at best."

"C'mon, man! Don't leave me hanging."

Bill was quiet for a minute. "Well look," he said, "a traveler story is incomplete by itself. The bulk of the story is about the journey, not the destination. A traveler can just be an aimless drifter—someone who goes from one episode to the next without any real sense of purpose in life. But part of your story is that you actually want that sense of purpose. You want to know about your destination."

"You mean wisdom?"

"Yes, from what I can tell, you've been trying to find your way to wisdom. Two thousand years ago, Aristotle was a traveler on the same road. He sketched a rough map of the terrain and passed that map on to others. They made additions and corrections to it and handed it on to yet others who did the same. And a version of that map made its way into my hands, and now I'm sharing it with you. So if I had to make a suggestion about next steps, I'd say learn more about Aristotle's philosophy."

# 7

"I'm curious," I said. "Why don't more people know about Aristotle's philosophy?"

"There are a few reasons," Bill said. "One is that Aristotle's surviving works are hard to read."

"What do you mean surviving?"

"Aristotle was writing over a thousand years before the printing press. Back then, if you wanted to copy a written document, you had to do it by hand—a slow, painstaking process. So at any given time there were only so many copies of an original document—maybe only one copy. If a fire or flood or some other disaster destroyed that copy, the document was lost to history forever. That's what happened to most of Aristotle's published works. All we have left are lecture notes and rough drafts. They're dense and not much fun to read. Even professional philosophers struggle to work through them. It's really too bad. Cicero was familiar with Aristotle's published works—including Aristotle's dialogues. He says Aristotle's prose was even better than Plato's. That's high praise coming from Cicero, especially because Plato's Greek is very nice. Second, I think a lot of people dismiss Aristotle because he got a bad rap."

"What do you mean?"

"Aristotle made a lot of scientific claims we now know to be false. He didn't have the experimental methods we have now or observational tools like microscopes or telescopes. So the scientific theories he developed were inaccurate in exactly the ways you'd expect for somebody whose observational tools were so limited. That by itself wouldn't have been a problem, but during the sixteenth and seventeenth centuries there was a lot of ideological warfare between defenders of Aristotle's science and its attackers. Those attackers included architects of the Scientific Revolution like Galileo. They won the war over Aristotle's science, but in the process Aristotle's philosophy suffered collateral damage."

"I'm not sure what you mean," I said.

"Back then, people didn't clearly distinguish science from philosophy. In fact, the word 'scientist' wasn't even coined till the nineteenth century. Before that the people we would now call 'scientists' were called 'natural philosophers,' and the study of the natural world that we would now call 'science' was called 'natural philosophy.' But the label 'natural philosophy' didn't apply only to what we would now call 'science.' It also applied to a lot of other things that we would now properly call 'philosophy.' So people didn't have a clear concept of the difference between science and philosophy. As a result, they didn't clearly distinguish Aristotle's philosophy from Aristotle's science. From their perspective, there was just this one thing: Aristotle's natural philosophy. They didn't distinguish the scientific bits from the philosophical bits.

"Architects of the Scientific Revolution were right that Aristotle's science was wrong in all sorts of respects. But because they didn't distinguish Aristotle's scientific claims from his philosophical claims—because they lumped claims of both sorts together under the one heading of natural philosophy—they ended up rejecting not just Aristotle's science but Aristotle's philosophy too. If they'd been as familiar with the distinction between science and philosophy as we are today, they might have realized that their real target was Aristotle's science. But because they weren't familiar with that distinction, they took themselves to be falsifying Aristotle's natural philosophy as a whole—not just the scientific parts, but all of it.

"One downstream effect of this history is that when you mention Aristotle to people today, a lot of them are instantly dismissive: 'Oh, his ideas were proven false hundreds of years ago.' That's what I mean when I say Aristotle got a bad rap. People don't realize that it was Aristotle's scientific ideas that were falsified. His philosophical ideas weren't falsified so much as ignored, forgotten, misrepresented, or misunderstood."

"That history explains a lot," I said. "But I just realized something."

"What's that?" Bill said.

"You never answered my earlier question."

"Which question?"

"How do I become wise? You said it takes reflection—that I've got to try to understand who I am and what my place in the world is, and that's an ongoing process. I think I get that. But what I don't get is… I suppose I still don't understand what wisdom is."

"Wisdom is a virtue," Bill said. "It's excellence in decision-making—the ability to judge correctly what kinds of things are worth pursuing in life and how best to pursue them. It's the ability to judge correctly what activities and abilities contribute to living well, and to think, feel, and act in line with those judgments."

"Wait, wisdom is an ability?"

"Yes, it's a virtue, and virtues are abilities. Think again of the sports analogy. What is knowing how to play basketball well? It's an ability to know in particular situations whether to dribble, or shoot, or fake, or pass, or press—and then to do exactly those things at the right time, in the right manner, for the right reasons. If you have that ability and use it, you end up playing the game well. Similarly, if you have wisdom—if you know and have the virtues it takes to live well and use them—then you end up thinking, feeling, and acting in the right ways, at the right times, in the right manner, and for the right reasons. And that's exactly what living well is."

"But," I said, "that's not… it still doesn't tell me… like when I asked, 'What is wisdom?' I was expecting you to say something like, 'It's this!' And you'd tell me something that would suddenly… I dunno… make everything clear to me. And I'd be like, 'Now I have wisdom. Now I know the secret.'"

"The secret about what?" Bill said.

"The secret about… I dunno… like… what's really important in life."

"Let's try this again," Bill said. "Suppose I ask you to tell me how to play great basketball, and you say, 'Playing basketball is a complex activity, so to do it well, you have to acquire and use this and that ability.' And I say, 'No, that doesn't tell me what I want. I want to know how to do it.' And you say, 'I just told you how to do it: it's a matter of using certain abilities, and to acquire those abilities you've got to practice.' And I say, 'No, no, no, you don't understand. That's not the answer I'm looking for. What I want is for you to tell me something—to say something to me that I can just know, and that'll make me a great player.' At that point, you've got to say something like, 'Knowing how to play great basketball isn't some fact that I can just state and you can just memorize. It's not something that's said. It's something that's done—a complex activity that uses the abilities to dribble, and pass, and shoot, and so on. To play basketball—and to play it well—you have to master those abilities. Telling you things—giving you words—isn't going to magically give you those abilities. The only way to get them is to practice.' Something analogous is true of wisdom. It's an ability—one of those very general abilities that Aristotle calls virtues. Becoming wise isn't a matter of someone telling you something—giving you words you can recite. It's a matter of practice."

"I think I get the point about practice," I said. "It's just… I dunno… I don't know exactly what I'm trying to say."

Bill was quiet for a moment. "I have a theory," he said. "Maybe this will help. Every day you encounter all sorts of people claiming to have the secret to this or that—the secret to making a fortune, the secret to six-pack abs, the secret to a happy marriage. Some even say, 'We've got the secret to life. We've discovered what it is and can share it with you if you just buy our product, or join our program, or sign up for our emails,' or whatever. Most of these claims you dismiss. But even though you dismiss them, they still affect how you think.

"You look at all these people in human history who have done great things—famous scientists, or musicians, or authors, or explorers—and you think, 'What did they have that made them great?' And you think maybe there's something you can learn that'll make you great like they were—some secret knowledge hidden in a vault somewhere in the world—knowledge that will give you the power to do amazing things and make everything in your life the way you want it—if you only have the key. And when it comes to imagining that secret knowledge, the sheer volume of people claiming to know the secret to this or that gets you thinking that if there is a secret to life, it's got to be something that can be communicated in words.

"So now when you and I get to talking about life and wisdom, you have in mind this mythology about secret knowledge. And when I say, 'Wisdom isn't something that can just be stated. It's an ability like being able to play great basketball,' what I say doesn't match your preconception of what wisdom is supposed to be. It's not a verbal message that I can just say, and you can just know. And because that account of wisdom doesn't match the mythic idea of wisdom you've inherited from the surrounding culture, you feel as though something is off. But what's off isn't the account of wisdom and life. What's off is the way you've been taught to think about wisdom and life. That's my theory. What do you think?"

"I don't know what to think."

"Okay. Think of it this way: if somebody said, 'Hey, Vishal, we've discovered the secret to playing great basketball. You don't have to practice, you don't have to do drills, you don't have to get in shape—nothing like that. All you have to do is know this thing that we'll tell you, and you can be as great as Michael Jordan or LeBron James.' What would you think?"

"I'd think they were full of shit."

"Exactly," Bill said. "When it comes to basketball, you know there isn't a hidden vault with secret knowledge that'll magically make you a great player. You know that basketball is a matter of ability, and that you don't get that ability without a lot of practice and hard work. What's true of basketball is true of any other complex activity: performing it well takes a lot of practice and hard work. It's absurd to suppose that you can get good just by having someone tell you something. Yet what strikes people as so absurd in these other cases somehow doesn't strike them as absurd when it comes to life. But how could life be different? How could any complex activity be different?"

"Do you think," I said, "that maybe people just don't think of life as a complex activity?"

"I think that's part of it," Bill said. "I also think there's a general human tendency to want there to be a secret to life. We encounter all sorts of hardships in life, and amid those hardships we just want something to make us well. Then someone comes around and promises to do that, and we want to believe them. We want to believe that there's a message or formula that'll just make everything right. There's actually a term for this tendency in human thought: gnosticism. You see it in all sorts of different forms throughout human history—from the Eleusinian mysteries in ancient Greece, to the plot lines of films like

*Raiders of Lost Ark* and *The DaVinci Code*. All of them touch on the gnostic desire for secret knowledge that'll solve all life's problems.

"And of course there are lots of people eager to exploit that desire. Stoicism, Scientology, psychedelics, self-help books—these and so many other things try to sell you on the idea that there's some secret knowledge that'll make everything right in your life. But there is no secret to life. If you try finding one, you'll end up believing one empty promise after another and run into Macbeth's problem.

"Wisdom isn't a secret teaching. It's an ability to think, feel, and act in ways that contribute to living well. It's not knowledge but know-how—a practiced sense of what really matters in life. There's no secret, no shortcut to becoming wise—no product to buy, no rule to follow, no life hack to try. There's no shortcut to getting better at any complex activity: not sports, not music, not friendship, not money, not marriage, not fitness, and not life. It takes hard work. Anyone who says otherwise is just trying to sell you something."

Bill and I had been talking for over an hour. I realized I no longer felt anxious or afraid. I stepped outside. The air was cool, the sky clear and bright above the distant mountains. "Why am I only learning about Aristotle now?" I said.

"I can't say exactly," Bill said. "Why are you asking?"

"I was just thinking… It's taken decades of my life to get to this conversation. When I look back at the road I've taken—so many wrong turns—I think I might've done better if I'd known about Aristotle sooner. I think of my father—of important things he never told me. He was curious about wisdom, but I don't think he worked at finding it. Now I'm a father. I don't want to make the same mistake with my kids. I guess… I guess I have a chance to course correct one more time for their sakes. And now I feel as though I have a map of the terrain—that rough map handed down from Aristotle. I don't fully understand how to use it yet, but I want to learn." I thanked Bill for helping me. "Let's talk more about Aristotle soon, please," I said, and got off the phone.

I came back to Michelle. I told her I wanted our vacation to end. "I'm going to die," I said, "not now, but someday. I don't want to squander whatever time we have." I wanted to get back to our kids.

In sports, there's always the hope of next season. I was ready for the next season of my life.

# JOIN TEAM ARISTOTLE!

askaristotle.xyz

# Credits

**Written by**
Vishal Sharma
William Jaworski

**Edited by**
Ellen Fishbein

**Designed by**
Sam Nightengale
Daniel R. Patierno
Drew Townsend
William Jaworski

**Printed by**
Texas Bindery

**Produced by**
Altamira Studio

**www.altamira.studio**